If you were me and lived in...
GREECE

A Child's Introduction to Culture Around the World

Carole P. Roman

Dedicated to Henia and Felix.

Special thanks to Chris K. at On Parade Diner.

ISBN: 1497526183
ISBN 13: 9781497526181

Library of Congress Control Number: 2014906478
CreateSpace Independent Publishing Platform
North Charleston, South Carolina

GREECE

ATHENS

If you were me and lived in Greece (Gree-se), you would find yourself in Southern Europe in a country that is located at the crossroads of Europe, Western Asia, and Africa. Greece is also known as the Hellenic Republic and has always been referred to as Hellas (Hel-las).

You might live in the capital, Athens (Atthenz). Athens is 3,400 years old and the largest city in Greece. It is an important city and has often been called the "cradle of western civilization." It has earned that name because it is the birthplace of democracy (dem-o-cra-cee). Democracy is a government run by many people rather than a single ruler.

Thousands of years ago, important teachers like Plato (Pl-ate-o) and Aristotle (Ar-ris-totel) had schools there. Many of their lessons are still taught in schools today.

If you were born in Greece, your parents might have picked Georgios (Geeg-org-os), Dimitrios (Dim-me-tree-os), or Nikolaos (Nik-kay-los) if you are a boy. If you are a girl, they could have chosen Eleni (E-len-ee), Sophia (So-fee-a), or Katerina (Kat- a- reen-a).

You know Mama (Ma-ma) and Baba (Ba-ba) are the ones who chose your name. Baba is how you would say daddy.

If you were me, you are probably named for your grandfather or grandmother who you call Papou (Pa-poo) and Ya-ya (Ya-ya).

8

Yaya would tell you stories about the drachmas (drak-mas) she used to buy food when she was a child. Today you would use a euro (ur-ro) to purchase things in the market. You might use yours to buy a pretty koukla (kook-la). Can you guess what that is?

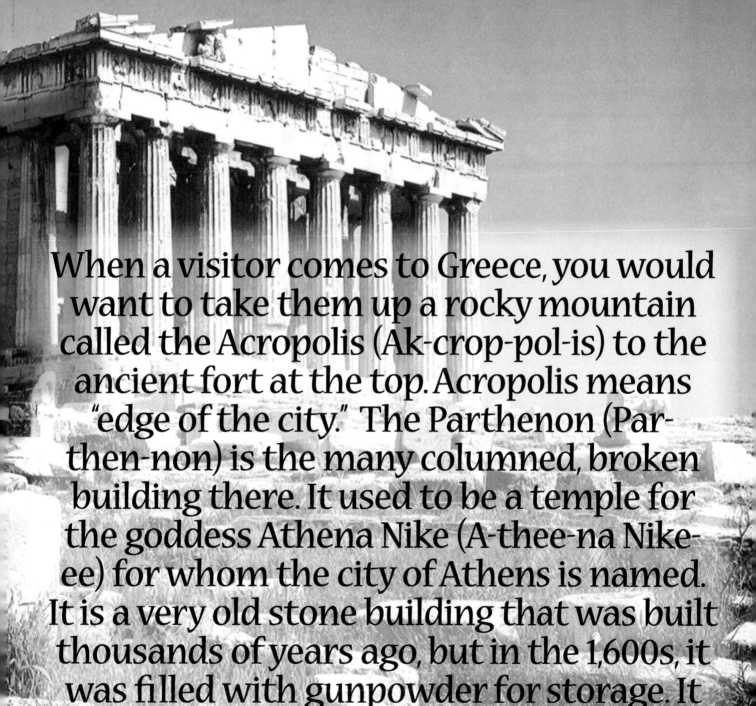

When a visitor comes to Greece, you would want to take them up a rocky mountain called the Acropolis (Ak-crop-pol-is) to the ancient fort at the top. Acropolis means "edge of the city." The Parthenon (Par-then-non) is the many columned, broken building there. It used to be a temple for the goddess Athena Nike (A-thee-na Nike-ee) for whom the city of Athens is named. It is a very old stone building that was built thousands of years ago, but in the 1,600s, it was filled with gunpowder for storage. It was hit by an enemy cannonball and was mostly destroyed.

Afterwards, you would go down the hill to Athens for a meal of fresh stuffed grape leaves, salad, and tzatziki (za-zeek-kee) sauce. Tzatziki is a tangy sauce made from yogurt and cucumber to put on roasted lamb. You might love the freshly-caught, grilled octopus and helloumi (hel-loom-ee) or grilled slabs of white cheese. You will always ask to finish your meal with loukoumades (loo-ka-mad-es), which is a doughnut covered with honey and cinnamon.

Everyday at the Parliament Building at eleven in the morning, there is an amazing ceremony of the changing of the guards. You would love to watch their synchronized movements and the wonderful uniforms with the white kilts and pompoms on their feet.

While soccer, or as you would call it "football," is a very important sport, everyone in Greece loves the Olympics. The Olympic Games were created in the town of Olympia (O-lim-pee-ya), Greece, in the eighth century BC. It was a huge athletic festival celebrating the best athletes from every town in the area. It is said that when they created the games, it caused the wars to often stop so they could compete instead.

The Feast of St. Basil (Bay-sil) would be one of your special holidays. It is an old Byzantine (Bis-in-teen) holiday to signify the start of the new year and called Casto Vassilopit (Cas-to Vas-sil-let-ta). You would hope to be the lucky one who gets the hidden coin in the Basil cake. This would mean that you would have good luck in the new year.

When you get back to sklayoh (sko-lay-oh), you will want to see who else found the lucky coin.

So you see, if you were me, how life in Greece
could really be.

24

Pronunciation Guide

Acropolis (Ak-crop-pol-is)-ancient fort high on a hill in Athens, Greece.

Aristotle (Ar-ris-tot-el)-famous teacher in ancient Greece.

Athena Nike (A-thee-na Nike-ee)-Goddess of wisdom.

Athens (At-thenz)-capital of Greece.

Baba (Ba-ba)-Daddy.

Byzantine (Bis-in-teen)-a style identified with ancient Greece.

Casto Vassilopit (Cas-to Vas-sil-let-a)-New Year.

democracy(dem-o-cra-cee)-a government ruled by the people.

Dimitrios (Dim-me-tree-os)-popular boy's name.

drachmas (drak-mas)-ancient money in Greece.

Eleni (E-len-ee)-popular girl's name.

euro (ur-ro)-currency used by most of Europe.

Georgios (Geeg-org-os)-popular boy's name.

Greece (Gree-se)-country in Southern Europe.

Hellas(Hel-las)-the ancient name for Greece.

helloumi (hel-loom-ee)-hard white cheese.

Katerina (Kat-a-reen-a)-popular girl's name.

koukla (kook-la)-doll.

loukoumades (loo-ka-mad-es)-doughnuts.

Mama (Ma-ma)-Mommy.

Nikolaos (Nik-kay-los)-popular boy's name.

Olympia (O-lim-pee-ya)-town in Greece where Olympics was born.

Papou (Pa-poo)-Grandpa.

Parthenon (Par-then-non)-building at the top of the Acropolis.

Plato (Pl-ate-o)-famous teacher in ancient Greece.

sklayoh (sko-lay-oh)-school.

Sophia (So-fee-a)-popular girl's name.

St. Basil (Bay-sil)-Saint Basil.

tzatziki (za-zeek-kee)-yogurt and cucumber mix used on lamb.

Ya-ya (Ya-ya)-Grandma.

Made in the USA
Charleston, SC
04 February 2015